Immigrants in Wales during the 20ᵗʰ century

Robin Evans

Contents

CW00429013

Published by CAA, University of Wales Aberystwyth, The Old College, King Street, Aberystwyth, SY23 2AX (http://www.caa.aber.ac.uk). Sponsored by the Welsh Assembly Government.

ISBN   978-1-84521-150-9

Editor: Gwenda Lloyd Wallace
Designer: Richard Huw Pritchard
Printers: Cambrian Printers

Acknowledgements
Thank you to the following for permission to reproduce materials in this publication:

Cover photographs: Photolibrary Wales, Butetown History and Arts Centre, Barry Johnston, India Dance Wales

Swansea Museum: p. 3(b)
National Museum of Wales: p. 7(l), 10(b), 16
The National Archives, Kew: p. 2 and 3 (t,l) (original crew lists), 6
BBC Cymru/Wales (*Week In, Week Out*, 8 June 1999): p. 45
Bernard Baldwin MBE: p. 12
John Briggs: p. 28(c), 30
Butetown History and Arts Centre: p. 22(b), 23
Edda Conti, widow of Ino Conti, Treharris: p. 20(l)
Corbis: p. 17, 49(b,l)
Ron Davies: p. 28(b)
Vivian Davies: p. 12 (extract from *These Poor Hands*, B.L. Coombes, Victor Gollancz, 1939)
Huw Evans Picture Agency Ltd.: p. 39(b,l)
Free Press and Rhondda Leader, 15 June 1940: p. 21
Fflic for S4C: p. 48(b,l)
Getty Images: p. 9(b), 13(b)
Guido Generale degli Italiani in Gran Bretagne, London, 1939: p. 20(r)
Wrexham Archives Service: p. 5(b)
Merthyr Tydfil Public Library Service: p. 5(t)
University of Wales Press: p. 13 (extract from *The Fed: A History of the South Wales Miners in the Twentieth Century*, Hywel Francis and David Smith, 1998); p. 43(b) (extract from *A Tolerant Nation?: exploring ethnic diversity in Wales*, Charlotte Williams, Neil Evans and Paul O'Leary, 2003); p. 26, 36 and 37 (extract from *Cymru 2000: Hanes Cymru yn yr Ugeinfed Ganrif*, R. Merfyn Jones, 1999)
Colin Hughes: p. 39(t)
India Dance Wales: p. 49(c)
Barry Johnston: p. 14(l)
Mike Jones: p. 29(b,r)
Gerallt Llewelyn: p. 35(c), 50
Llwybr Llaethog: p. 48(b,l)
National Library of Wales: p. 25, 28(t)
Cardiff Public Library: p. 11
By permission of Rhondda Cynon Taf Libraries: p. 4
Mirrorpix: p. 20(b) (*Daily Mirror*, 27 April 1940)
Keith Morris: p. 27(l)
National Maritime Museum, Greenwich: p. 3 (original list for SS Straits of Menai)
Pablo Photographics: p. 31
Photolibrary Wales: p. 13(t), 27(t), 35(t), 36, 37(t), 38(t), 39(b,r), 41, 43, 47, 48(t)
Rex Features: p. 46(b,l)
Tegwyn Roberts: p. 10(r), 22(t,r)
Dr Vaughan Robinson: p. 42
Sain: p. 49(t,r)
David H. Smith: p. 14(r)
Janet Ryder's Constituency Office, Ruthin: p. 37(b)
Tate, London 2006/Renate Koppel: p. 16(t)
Topfoto: p. 19, 22(t,l), 27(b,r), 29(t and b,l), 34, 46(t,r and b,r)
Western Mail & Echo: p. 7(r), 9(l), 46(t,l and c)
Nia Wyn Williams: p. 18
Charlotte Williams: p. 49(t,l)
Winvest: p. 38(graphs)

Thank you to Richard Evans, Ian Farquharson, Davyth Fear, Gillian Hayward, Bethan James, John Leung, Alun Morgan, Paul O'Leary, Vicky Owen, Siân Pugh and Alan Roberts for their valuable guidance.

Thank you to the following schools for taking part in the trialling process:

Ysgol Dyffryn Conwy, Llanrwst
Duffryn High School, Newport
Cathays High School, Cardiff
Cefn Hengoed Community School, Swansea

Also available is *Mewnfudwyr yng Nghymru yn ystod yr 20fed Ganrif*, a Welsh medium version of this publication.

Introduction

The world comes to Wales

The documents below list the crew members of ships belonging to the Jenkins Brothers company of Cardiff during the early 20th century. You will notice that the crews were made up of men from different nationalities. Due to the nature of their work, sailors from different nationalities could be found all over the world. That is why it was possible to find sailors from Wales in ports in South America, the USA, China, Africa, Australia … in all parts of the world.

The ports of Wales were some of the busiest in the world. Coal from South Wales was exported through ports such as Cardiff and Barry, coal from North Wales through Point of Ayr, tinplate and coal through Swansea, and slate was exported from ports such as Porthmadog and Bangor. This activity was due to the Industrial Revolution, when Wales became one of the most important industrial countries in the world. The population of Wales grew as people migrated here in search of work. By 1900, people from many different countries lived in Wales.

The crew of S.S. Glamorgan, September 1914

Name	Residence	Position	Age
J.P. Jones	Beulah	Captain	47
G. Davies	Aber-porth	1st Mate	27
R. Lloyd	Nefyn	2nd Mate	28
John Williams	Porthmadog	Bosun	46
Albert Richards	Aberdyfi	A.B.	35
D. Morris	Cardigan	O.S.	21
W. Morris	St. Dogmaels	O.S.	23
K. Trykina	Cardiff (Norway)	A.B.	27
E. Martinsen	Cardiff (Norway)	O.S.	25
F. Chagnon	Aber-porth	O.S.	15
Isaac Evans	Llan-non	O.S.	18
Thomas Venables	South Shields	1st Engineer	44
D. Francis	Dinas Cross	2nd Engineer	31
E. Hooton	Llandaff	3rd Engineer	25
G. Davies	Penarth	4th Engineer	21
J. Hastie	Blyth	Donkeyman	40
C. Libante	Cardiff (St. Kitts-Nevis)	Fireman	23
W. Packling	Cardiff (St. Kitts-Nevis)	Fireman	27
W. Henry	Cardiff (Bermuda)	Fireman	29
R. Dulcie	Cardiff (St. Lucia)	Fireman	21
J. Griffith	Cardiff (Barbados)	Fireman	30
M. Lynch	Cardiff (St. Lucia)	Fireman	29
J. Thomas	Barry	Fireman	25
G. Kent	North Shields	Steward	50
F.W. Blythe	Tal-y-waun	Captain's Steward	20
N. Campbell	Belfast	Cook	37
K. Olafsen	Cardiff (Norway)	A.B.	45

The crew of S.S. Farringford, March 1914.

Name	Residence	Position	Age
T.L. Davies	Dinas Cross	Captain	31
F. Foley	Aberafan	1st Mate	46
W.M. Evans	Aberaeron	2nd Mate	38
T.M. Thomas	Aber-porth	Bosun	36
T.Ll. Davies	New Quay	A.B.	27
F.W. Hardwick	Barry	A.B.	20
M. Allen	Cardiff (Ireland)	O.S.	21
J. O'Leary	Cardiff (Ireland)	A.B.	23
M. McCarthy	Cardiff (Ireland)	A.B.	28
Joseph Leary	Cardiff (Ireland)	O.S.	21
J.L. James	Aber-porth	O.S.	15
S.R. Davies	Cwm-cou	1st Engineer	28
H. Vaughan	Cardiff	2nd Engineer	33
Thomas Meredith	Morriston	3rd Engineer	22
O. Negard	Cardiff (Norway)	Donkeyman	41
C. Isaac	Cardiff (St. Kitts-Nevis)	Fireman	43
J.H. Johnson	Virginia U.S.A.	Fireman	38
R. Bechoras	Cardiff (Spain)	Fireman	27
E. Aldominez	Cardiff (Spain)	Fireman	46
A. Hernacles	London (Greece)	Fireman	23
C.A. Carlson	Cardiff (Sweden)	Fireman	32
E. Rees	Aber-porth	Steward	53
John J. Rees	Aber-porth	Captain's Steward	15
T. Vautier	Southampton	Cook	50

The crew of S.S. Italiana, May 1916			
Name	Residence	Position	Age
Hugh Roberts	Nefyn	Captain	62
D.J. Evans	Llanon	1st Mate	30
R.G. Davies	Fishguard	2nd Mate	52
W. Parker	Barry	Bosun	42
J. Manning	London	O.S.	22
J. Burns	Penarth	A.B.	34
G.T. Lewis	Aberaeron	O.S.	23
Jenkin Evans	Llanon	A.B.	44
G. Gregory	Plymouth	O.S.	26
L. John	Barry	O.S.	22
John Brown	Aber-porth	O.S.	16
John Sampson	Liverpool	1st Engineer	57
C. Griffiths	Pontnewydd	2nd Engineer	32
W.D. Jones	Swansea	3rd Engineer	36
S. Harding	Cardiff	Donkeyman	57
Abdulla Mahomed	Cardiff (Arab)	Fireman	29
Abdul Assis	Cardiff (Arab)	Fireman	36
Nasir Ali	Cardiff (Arab)	Fireman	29
Rahmin Nahli	Cardiff (Arab)	Fireman	21
Abdullah Mohamed	Cardiff (Arab)	Fireman	22
Jaheh Ahmed	Cardiff (Arab)	Fireman	21
William Jones	Borth	Steward	25
W.S. Seed	Swansea	Cook	26
D.J. Gray	Cardigan	Captain's Steward	15

The crew of S.S. Straits of Menai, November 1904			
Name	Residence	Position	Age
E.T. Elias	Bethesda	Captain	33
D. Davies	Newport, Pembrokeshire	1st Mate	48
D.J. Davies	Llan-non	2nd Mate	23
J. Roberts	Cricieth	Steward	45
A. Pearce	London	Cook	31
E. Wilson	West Hartlepool	Captain's Steward	16
L.H. Lammy	Cardiff	Bosun	22
P. Borgitos	Cardiff (Greece)	A.B.	35
G. Arnold	Cardiff	A.B.	49
W. Fitzgerald	London	A.B.	43
James Lucas	Cardiff	A.B.	30
James Gillespie	Cardiff	A.B.	26
Lucas Kerz	Cardiff (Germany)	A.B.	32
W. Brown	Cardiff	1st Engineer	44
A. Davies	Cardiff	2nd Engineer	30
A. Hemmingway	Cardiff	3rd Engineer	23
M. Giovanni	Cardiff (Italian)	Donkeyman	25
H.J. Edward	Cardiff	Fireman	25
H. Rogers	Cardiff	Fireman	24
A. Dunovich	Cardiff (Hungary)	Fireman	26
T. Morrison	Cardiff	Fireman	26
E. Kinney	Cardiff (Ireland)	Fireman	38

Key:
A.B. – Able-bodied Seaman
O.S. – Ordinary Seaman
Donkeyman – in charge of the donkey engine.

Study the crew lists again and consider the following questions:

- Apart from Wales, from where did the crew members come?
- Would some of them have settled in Wales?
- From which towns and villages in Wales did the crew members come?
- Is there a pattern at all?

In this book you will read about the experiences of different immigrants in twentieth century Wales. You will see that different people have moved here at different times and for different reasons. Some were immediately accepted in their new communities, others faced problems. In the long run, all of them contributed to life in Wales and played an important part in the country's history.

People from all over the world could be found in ports such as Swansea

People on the move

Over the centuries, people have migrated for many different reasons. Remember, some of the causes of migration never change. For example:

- People have often moved to escape from war, even if only for a brief period.
- Others left their homes forever in search of work and a new life elsewhere.
- Over the centuries, famine has often been a serious problem for people in several parts of the world, and the only chance of survival for many was to move elsewhere.
- People have often had to escape to save their lives because they were being persecuted for their religion, their political beliefs or their race.

 Look carefully at the above reasons for migration. Can you think of specific examples from different periods in history and from different parts of the world?

Many Welsh people have also left their homeland for a number of reasons:

- Many Welshmen fought alongside the Normans and the English in Ireland and France during the Middle Ages – some out of choice, others because they were forced to.
- During the age of Elizabeth I (1558-1603), a number of Welsh Catholics went to live in Spain, France and Italy because they were being persecuted. They hoped to return to Wales once the country was Catholic again!
- Some migrated to Patagonia in South America during the 19th century in order to live their lives completely through the Welsh language. They did not intend returning to Wales.
- One of Italy's most famous artists was Llewelyn Lloyd. His family were Welsh merchants who had set up their business in the port of Livorno in Italy, and it was there that Llewelyn was born in 1879.
- The United States has been a popular destination for Welsh migrants over the last two hundred years … but the country which has been the main attraction for Welsh migrants over the centuries is England!

Wales is a country of immigrants!

Did you know that the first Welshmen were immigrants to Wales! Then, at different times over the centuries, the Romans, the Irish, the Normans, the English and the Flemish moved to Wales in large numbers. Gypsies and Jews have also played an important part in Welsh history. Many individuals from various countries around the world have moved here too – some permanently, others for a short period only. Some immigrants came to look for work, while others, like the Huguenots (French Protestants), came to escape persecution in their own country.

The greatest wave of immigrants came to Wales in the 19th century, due to the Industrial Revolution. The population of South Wales in particular grew quickly as people moved there in search of work. The South Wales valleys attracted Welsh speaking and English speaking Welshmen and Welshwomen. From outside Wales came the English and the Irish, but they were not the only immigrants – many people from other parts of the world arrived in Wales in search of work and a better life.

William Haggar, originally from England. He brought film and the travelling cinema to South Wales.

Industrial towns such as Merthyr Tydfil attracted immigrants from other parts of Wales, from the rest of the British Isles and from Europe

Population of Wales in 1891:
1,771,451

Brymbo Steelworks, near Wrexham

Chapter 1 1900-1918

Overview

By the beginning of the twentieth century the world was changing rapidly. Developments in shipping, among other factors, led to growth and development in international trade. Due to industrialisation, Wales was an important centre of the world's economy. Competition between the large trading nations of the world was one of the causes of the First World War, which had such a great effect on communities in Wales and beyond. The many changes that took place in Wales and the wider world had an effect on the various people of Wales – on the Welsh themselves, on traditional immigrants and on the new immigrants.

The Irish

The Welsh and the Irish have been neighbours for centuries and there have been many links between the two countries, including religious and trading links.

During the 19th century, and much of the 20th century, the Irish experienced large scale emigration. Poverty and famine in Ireland were the main reasons for Irish emigration during the 19th century. Between 1845 and 1850, one million people died during the Great Famine in Ireland and over one million Irish men, women and children emigrated. The majority moved to the United States and England, but a large number also arrived in Wales. Even though they did not receive a warm welcome everywhere, and there were anti-Irish riots at times, by the beginning of the twentieth century there were 20,000 Irish people living in Wales. On the whole, they went to live in the large towns, including Merthyr Tydfil and Cardiff. Many went to Cardiff to work as labourers building the docks. The poorer Irish were squeezed into a corner of Cardiff called Newtown. This area became known as 'Little Ireland'.

Immigrants from Ireland were not always warmly welcomed in Wales, as this poster from the nineteenth century shows

Most of the Irish were Catholic, but most of the Welsh were Protestant. Irish immigration therefore had an effect on the religious make-up of Wales and meant that the Irish were not welcomed by all. Due to the large number of Irish immigrants, a Catholic College was established in Holywell in 1904 so that Catholic priests could learn Welsh and spread Catholicism in Wales. So many Catholics moved to Wales that the Catholic Church established an archbishopric in Wales in 1916. Cardiff's first Catholic Archbishop was James Bilsborrow, from England.

Building Roath Dock, April 1884, where many of the Irish were employed

Paul Radmilovic. A Welsh and international swimming champion. His mother was Irish and his father Greek.

Gypsies

Gypsies (the Roma) had been a part of Welsh, and European life, for centuries. They had a unique way of life, and their own language and traditions. As a result, they were often seen as outsiders and not always welcomed when they set up camp in a locality.

This was the case in Barmouth in 1901 when a local newspaper stated that the Gypsies' camp should be destroyed and the Gypsies sent on their way. In one journal in 1914, the Gypsies responded, and one Gypsy, Eli Burton, stated that people needed to be educated about the Gypsies' way of life – that is, that not all Gypsies were thieves or murderers! He also said that all towns should have sites with modern conveniences for Gypsies.

Was Eli Burton correct – in order for people to understand one another, education is the answer?

The Jews

The Jews have been both welcomed and persecuted across Europe at different times. They were an important part of Welsh life because travelling Jews visited isolated villages across Wales, selling a variety of goods.

In 1900, an article in *Y Clorianydd*, an Anglesey newspaper, started a debate. The article was entitled '*Pla yr Iddewon*' (The Jewish Plague) and listed complaints about travelling Jews:

'The Jewish Plague'

There are so many of them.
Local people cannot afford the goods on offer.
The local people who cannot pay are taken to court as debtors.
The travelling Jews sell their goods on Sundays.

The article also made it clear that it was only right that Jews be paid for their goods, and criticized the Welsh for their foolishness in buying goods that they did not need.

One of those who responded to the newspaper's criticism was Morris Wartski, a Jew who owned a shop in Bangor and who was well respected in the area. He emphasized that the Jews had been accepted locally, but he warned people to be wary of the travelling Jews!

By the early 20th century there were Jewish communities in Swansea, Tredegar, Bangor, Cardiff and Llanelli. These communities varied in size – there were around 2,000 Jews living in Cardiff and around 150 in Tredegar. In Cardiff, Jewish shops could be found in poor and wealthy areas. Jews did not work in the docks – they wanted to keep the Sabbath, and it was far easier to do so if they ran their own businesses and controlled their own work hours. On the other hand, there is evidence of Jews working as coalminers in Abertyswg.

There is no history of violence against Jews in Wales prior to the twentieth century, but in 1911 there were anti-Jewish riots in Tredegar.

THE 1911 RIOTS

The riots in Tredegar started just before midnight on Saturday 19th August 1911. A great deal of damage was done to Jewish property, and the police failed to stop the rioters. The trouble spread to other parts of the South Wales valleys, and two shops owned by Jews in Senghennydd were set on fire. As a result, the Jews left Tredegar.

Were they caused by economic problems?

1911 was a year of economic difficulties, and poor families were in debt to shopkeepers and landlords. Therefore shops were attacked because of high food prices, and landlords were attacked because people were in debt to them. Some of those landlords were Jews.

Some historians believe that the Tredegar riots were an example of economic protest in Wales.

Were they due to racism?

Some historians believe that the riots were racist – the only pogrom in the history of the British Isles – because:

- Properties belonging to the Jews were the first to be attacked.
- Although the rioters attacked property belonging to people who were not Jews, all Jewish property was attacked.

Yet, a number of local people succeeded in defending some of the Jews from the crowd. Some local people said that the rioters were hooligans from outside the locality.

A policeman guarding one of the Jewish shops in Tredegar, but too late

 Historians still disagree today whether or not the motive behind the riots was racism. What do you think? (Consider the above evidence, the other pages on the Jews in this book, and your own knowledge of the history of the Jews in Wales and Europe over the centuries.)

Wrecked shops boarded up

The bustling docks

As we saw at the beginning of this book, people from all over the world could be found in Welsh ports. One place which attracted migrants from many parts of the world before the First World War was Butetown in Cardiff, which was also called Tiger Bay. Tiger Bay was the docks area of Cardiff. As there were few people from different ethnic backgrounds living in the rest of Wales, there was a lot of ignorance and prejudice towards communities like Tiger Bay.

The Somalis

One ethnic group to arrive in Wales were the Somalis. They worked on ships sailing from Wales, and their aim was to make enough money to buy livestock back home. While in Cardiff, they stayed in lodgings run by Somalis who had settled in Wales. This was very convenient for them – they were staying with people who spoke the same language, had the same customs and were from a similar background.

The Norwegians

One of the world's major shipping countries was Norway, and so it's no surprise that many Norwegians made their homes in Cardiff. Many Norwegian businessmen lived there and owned shops or lodging houses. Many decided to stay and married locally.

Cardiff's Norwegian Church

Getting work on a ship was not easy – a sailor was hired for one voyage only and he was then

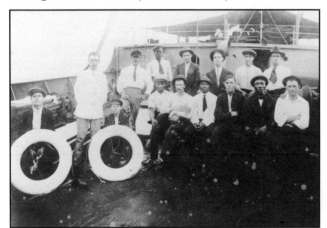

discharged or he signed on for another voyage. In docks all over the world, men from all races competed for work, and this sometimes led to conflict – between people of different nationalities or with different colour skin, but it could also happen between local people. This was particularly true during periods of economic depression.

Many Butetown inhabitants would sail on Welsh ships and several of them could therefore speak Welsh. The photograph shows the crew of the S.S. Glamorgan in Ibiza in 1913.

The Chinese

One ethnic group which could be found in port towns throughout the world were the Chinese. Around 200 Chinese lived in Cardiff, which was a very small number. They were either sailors or ran laundries, and they had established over 30 laundries across Cardiff. They were recognized as being hard-working people who were cheap to employ. While some people praised them for their hard work and the fact that they were law-abiding citizens, others were suspicious of them.

1910-11 was a period of industrial discontent in South Wales. In June 1911, a seamen's strike took place in Cardiff and led to attacks on property and violence. If the seamen's strike was to succeed, then the strikers had to be kept united. The Seamen's Union had already shown its anger at the Chinese who were willing to work for low wages and who kept out of trouble. Some believed, without any evidence, that they were persuading white women to be prostitutes and that they smoked opium. One aspect of such prejudice was that a request from Chinese seamen to join the union was refused.

An attack on the Chinese

Given this background, it's not surprising that one result of the dispute of 1911 was an attack on the Chinese in Cardiff.

When a crew of Chinese sailors arrived in port, the opportunity arose to attack them. Every single Chinese laundry in Cardiff was attacked and there was also physical violence against the Chinese. There is no doubt that they were being used as scapegoats (i.e. being deliberately blamed).

It can be argued that these attacks were:

- unusual – because there was no history of such attacks in Cardiff;
- racist – the Chinese were of a different colour, spoke a very different language and had different traditions;
- due to fear – sailors were scared of losing their jobs to foreign workers;
- deliberate – the Seamen's Union believed that an attack on one group of workers, i.e. the Chinese, would keep everyone who was part of the strike united;
- a combination of the above!

- What were the similarities and differences between the attacks on the Jews in Tredegar and the attacks on the Chinese in Cardiff during 1911?

- Why were there no attacks on Norwegian and Somali immigrants?

One of Cardiff's Chinese men being protected by the police during the 1911 disturbances

A Changing Wales

At the beginning of the twentieth century, 27% of the population of Glamorgan, Wales' most populous county, had been born outside Wales. Although those who came to Wales came from many different countries and settled in different parts of Wales, it was the industrial areas which attracted the majority. Some immigrant groups stood out more than others.

The English

16% of the population of Wales had been born in England, and the English who came to Wales contributed to the country in many ways, especially in the industrial working class areas. There was no conflict between the Welsh and the English as there was between other ethnic groups. Many of the English who came to Wales kept their traditions and identity, while others, within a generation or two, had become Welsh themselves. English became the main language of several communities at the expense of the Welsh language. The English who learnt to speak Welsh were a minority, even in those areas where the Welsh language was strong.

Here is how one miner described the racially mixed mining workforce of the Neath Valley:

'What a mixture of languages and dialects … Yorkshire and Durham men, Londoners, men from the Forest of Dean, North Welshmen … two Australians, four Frenchmen and several coloured gentlemen.
Of course, the Welshmen were at a disadvantage when they tried to convey their thoughts in … English.
The meetings had to be in English because most of the Welshmen could express themselves to some extent in English, while the majority of the English maintained a frightened silence whenever Welsh was spoken.'

The Italians

Many Italians came to live in Wales, mostly in the South. The first Italians arrived through the ports. Although some of them faced hostility at the beginning, they soon became accepted by the local community. Before long, there was not one village or town in South Wales which did not have an Italian café. They were welcomed by chapelgoers and churchgoers because they offered an alternative to public houses. The cafés were usually family businesses and the profits were sent home to Italy. Through working very hard for long hours, and by being careful with their money, the Italians could maintain a decent standard of living.

Number of people born in Italy and living in Wales 1881-1921					
County	1881	1891	1901	1911	1921
Glamorgan	445	511	684	833	997
Monmouth	89	31	89	303	335
Rest of Wales	36	25	153	159	201
Total	580	567	926	1295	1533

Giuseppe Rabaiotti with his ice cream cart in Mountain Ash around 1907

The Spanish

King Alfonso Street

A group of immigrants from northern Spain, especially the Basque Country, arrived in Merthyr Tydfil in 1907 to work in the local iron industry. By 1911 there were about 250 Spaniards living in the town. Some moved to Abercrave to work in the local coal mines, and soon there were around 200 Spaniards living there too. The street where they lived was called 'Spanish Row' or 'Espaniardos Row'. There is also a street in Dowlais called King Alfonso Street, which dates from the same period.

Some local chapel leaders were opposed to them because they were Catholics or atheists, and because they danced and sang and drank alcohol on the streets on a Saturday and Sunday night. Young people were more willing to accept them. Some of the Welsh and Spanish became such good friends that they learnt each other's language. David Smith and Hywel Francis describe it like this in their book *The Fed: A History of the South Wales Miners in the Twentieth Century*:

'... it was not uncommon to hear a Welsh collier shout from the coalface to a Spanish haulier: "Caballista! Uno caballo!" (Haulier! One horse!). The reply was likely to have been in Welsh or Spanish but not in English.'

Spaniards were not the only immigrants to work in the area. Frenchmen, Germans and Italians also worked there. By 1914 some local workers feared that the owners aimed to employ cheaper workers from abroad. The locals protested. In one case, local miners refused to go down the mines with the foreign workers. The leader of the foreign workers tried to defend the Spanish, arguing that they, like the local miners, were ordinary workers. It appears that there was a racist aspect to the protest, but it came to an end when the Great War broke out, which created work locally. At the end of the war, the Miners' Federation insisted that those who had gone home to fight should be allowed to return to their work in the coal mines.

Suggest reasons why some immigrant workers were welcomed in Wales more than others.

Sport for all

Many of the young Spaniards and Basques soon took part in local sports. Sport tells us a great deal about society at the time and attitudes towards immigrants. By the 20th century, sport had become an important part of people's lives, especially competitive sports. As some people now had more leisure time, going to watch sports also became very popular.

During the second half of the 19th century and early in the 20th century, rugby became Wales' national sport and attracted English and Irish players. William O'Neil, whose family came from Cork in Ireland, was capped eleven times for Wales between 1904 and 1908. When Wales defeated New Zealand in a rugby international in 1905, the team captain was Gwyn Nicholls, who was born in England! He was one of several Englishmen who contributed to the golden age of rugby in Wales at the turn of the twentieth century.

One of the most famous boxers of the period was 'Peerless' Jim Driscoll who was born in the 'Little Ireland' district of Cardiff in 1880. He won the Lonsdale Belt in 1910-11 and the Welsh recognized him as the 'Prince of Wales'. He was a devout Catholic, and refused to fight on one occasion as he had promised to visit a Catholic children's home in Cardiff.

Did developments in sport offer opportunities for immigrants from different ethnic backgrounds?

Jim Driscoll

The Great War (1914-1918)

During the Great War, millions of people died in countries across Europe. It was not possible to name all the dead, and thousands of bodies remain unaccounted for up to this day.

One of those to lose his life was the young soldier in the photograph below. All we know about him is that he came from Butetown in Cardiff. Although Cardiff's ethnic community was not large at the time, his death reminds us that people of all backgrounds, from all parts of Wales, fought in the war. The fact that we do not know his name reminds us of the horror of war. He was one of the 'unknown soldiers.'

Another man who died during the Great War, in 1917, on the field of battle in Belgium, was Adolphus Wood. He was one of the Welsh Gypsies and was famous throughout North Wales as he and his brother Cornelius travelled around playing their fiddles, which had been made out of old chocolate boxes.

Wars can cause huge problems for immigrants. Dr. Hermann Ethé was a lecturer at Aberystwyth University. He had left Germany to live in Wales in 1875 because he was opposed to the military policies of Germany. He was very popular at the university, but when the war started there were protests against Germans and other foreigners. A crowd marched to Dr. Ethé's home. He left Aberystwyth the following day. The same night, the crowd went to the home of Dr. Schott and he was told to leave the town. But the crowd had made a mistake. Dr. Schott was not German – he was English!

This sort of activity was not confined to one part of Wales – there was also an anti-German riot in Rhyl in 1915.

The unknown soldier from Butetown

A rare photograph of Adolphus and Cornelius Wood with their fiddles

The Belgians

Britain became involved in the Great War because Germany had attacked Belgium – Britain had an agreement with Belgium to help her if she was attacked. At the beginning of the war, there was a lot of public sympathy for the Belgians, and many came to live in Wales in order to escape from the German armed forces.

When the Belgian refugees arrived in Wales they were welcomed wherever they went. Many found refuge in Cardiff and all over South Wales. Several of them went to live in Swansea as there were already a number of Belgians employed in the metal industry there. The Belgians included famous writers and artists who raised money to help the refugees. Between 1914 and 1916, Belgian refugees built the promenade at Menai Bridge on Anglesey, which became known as the Belgian Promenade.

The British government had said that the war would be over in no time. However, it soon became apparent that this would not be the case. Some people started to complain that the Belgians should return home in order to fight against the Germans. Others were of the opinion that they should be working, but the South Wales Miners' Federation was worried by this idea because unemployment continued to be a problem in some areas in South Wales.

 Did war change the attitudes of the people of Wales towards immigrants?

Cause and Effect
*   Which groups of people moved to Wales during the period 1900-1918?
*   What were the reasons for this?
*   How did these groups contribute to the history of Wales during the period 1900-1918?

Glossary
emigrant – *ymfudwr*, someone who leaves his country for another country
ethnic immigrants – *mewnfudwyr ethnig*, people from different races or cultures who move into a country from another country
immigrant – *mewnfudwr*, someone who moves into a country from another country
in-migrant – *mewnfudwr*, someone who moves into an area from another area in the same country
migrant – *mudwr*, someone who migrates
to migrate – *mudo*, to move from one place to another, e.g. in order to live or to work
multicultural – *amlddiwylliannol*, a mixture of different languages, peoples, religions, cultures
out-migrant – *allfudwr*, someone who moves out of an area into another area in the same country
to persecute – *erlid*, harassing/picking on people for a variety of reasons
pogrom – *pogrom*, an organized massacre
prejudice – *rhagfarn*, an unfair opinion or feeling against people because you are suspicious of people who are different to you

Chapter 2 1918-1945

Overview: War and Depression

The period between the two world wars (1919–1939) was a period of economic depression. There was a great struggle for jobs throughout Wales. It's therefore of no surprise that thousands of people left Wales in search of work in various parts of England and beyond. Some historians believe that between 20% and 25% of the population of

Wales left the country during this period. There was, however, a number of people who migrated to Wales during this time too. Some arrived through the South Wales ports. Most were sailors, but some opened lodging houses in the ports. Partly because of events abroad, including the effects of the Second World War (1939–1945), many refugees arrived in Wales.

'Snow, Sunshine, Rain' by Heinz Koppel, the German expressionist painter who moved to Wales in the 1930s

The years immediately following the Great War (1914-1918) were very hard years. There were racist attacks in many parts of the British Isles. Cardiff was the main focus of these attacks in Wales, but there were also cases in Newport and Barry.

The Cardiff Riots 1919

The riots in Cardiff started with attacks on black men and their white wives, and on people of Chinese, Greek and Arab descent. Their property and lodgings were also attacked. The black men were willing to fight to defend themselves. A total of five people died during the riots. The authorities responded by arresting many of the black men. Around 200 were deported. The authorities said that they did this in order to protect the black men!

Some black men and their white wives in Cardiff

Causes of the conflict

During the First World War, the government, led by Lloyd George, had promised 'homes fit for heroes' once the war was over. However, because of economic hardship, the government was unable to keep its promise. Many people were disappointed. Were they now looking for someone to blame?

Most of the people who attacked the immigrants during the riots were sailors and soldiers who had returned home from the war. There were not many jobs for them. The white men who came home believed that, compared to them, the black men had lived an easy life during the war. But 1,000 black sailors from Cardiff were killed during the war.

Sailors came to Cardiff from all parts of Wales, Europe and beyond. On the one hand, they were used to working side by side at sea. On the other, divisions existed because of background, religion, race, language and other differences. Therefore, there was a great possibility of friction, especially during a period of economic depression.

Many black men worked in the docks. They were accepted by many locals. Some of them married white women and settled down in Cardiff. But this caused friction at times as some white people resented their presence.

Some people condemned the tactics but not the sentiment – that is, they supported the protest against immigrants but did not support the use of violence.

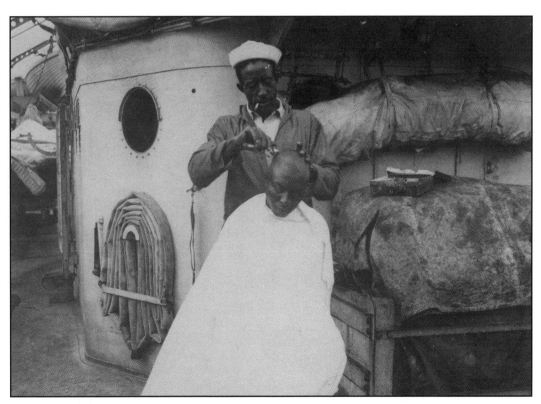

A black sailor having a haircut on board ship, c. 1914-1918

 In your view, was racism the cause of the riots?

The traditional immigrants

The immigrants of Tiger Bay, Cardiff were not the only ones who felt that they were different to the rest of the people of Wales.

The Irish

The Irish who had moved to Wales considered themselves different to the Welsh because they came from a different country and because of their Catholic religion. Their children and their children's children also considered themselves to be Irish even though they had never visited Ireland. There were many Irish Catholic communities in Wales. They were able to keep their separate identity due mainly to the Catholic faith. They had their own Catholic schools and their own Catholic rugby clubs. They were therefore promoting their own identity (i.e. keeping their Irish roots and way of life alive). This could sometimes lead to friction, as happened in Pembrokeshire during the 1930s when there was fighting between the Irish and the local community.

The Gypsies

The Gypsies, or the Roma, were another group that was considered different to the Welsh. Although they had been a part of Welsh history for centuries, many people regarded them as being different to the rest of society. By the 1920s, English had replaced Romanus as the language of most Gypsies, but they were still thought of as a group that was outside the rest of society. By this time, the Roma were a small network of families dotted here and there across the country. Although some of the Welsh Gypsies, such as the family of Abram Wood, could speak Welsh, they did not consider themselves to be Welsh or English. They lived at Betws Gwerful Goch in North Wales and spoke Welsh and English, and also a pure form of the old Roma language. This language had died out in several other areas of Europe.

Eldra Jarman, Gypsy historian and Welsh author, who was descended from the Wood family

An Englishman, Dr. John Sampson from Liverpool, studied the Gypsies' language and way of life and lived among them. The Gypsies had a great respect for him and called him 'tacho Phral' ('a true brother'). When Dr. Sampson died in 1931, his ashes were scattered over Foel Goch above the village of Llangwm. At his funeral, Welsh folk tunes were played by three Gypsy fiddlers, three generations of the same family, each one called Reuben Roberts.

The Jews

There were many Jewish communities in South Wales, including at Bryn-mawr, Newport, Merthyr, Aberdare and Swansea. There was more than one synagogue in Cardiff and they were important social centres. The wealthier Jews lived in Cathedral Road, while the rabbis and poorer Jews lived in Canton and Riverside. Jews were part of the wider community. Jewish children went to local schools and to the university. In 1928, the first Jewish councillor was elected to Cardiff Council.

Despite the Tredegar riots of 1911, there is no evidence that the Jews lived in fear of their neighbours. But, as an ethnic minority, they were eager to protect their religion, and they feared inter-marriage and assimilation (being made like the rest of society).

Alfred Mond, a German Jew and MP for Swansea 1910-24

The years between the two world wars saw many economic problems. The Great Depression hit the Jews hard, as it did most people in Wales. Contrary to what we might expect, the main effects of the depression on Jewish pawn shops was to destroy their trade. Orthodox Jews slowly began to leave the valleys in order to settle in Cardiff.

What evidence is there on these two pages that the Irish, the Gypsies and the Jews were accepted, and not accepted, by society?

The Italians

By the 1920s and the 1930s there was an Italian café in almost every town and village in South Wales. The cafés could also be found in some of Wales' seaside resorts, such as Aberystwyth. It was important for the Italians to be good businessmen, especially during a period of economic depression. Some would sell chips during the winter months, while others took advantage of the popularity of the cinemas to sell ice-cream there. They worked long hours in the cafés, from six in the morning until eleven at night. They were open seven days a week, throughout the year. By the end of the 1930s there were over 300 Italian cafés throughout Wales.

Luigi Conti's café in Aberfan during the early 1930s

Advertising an Italian café in 1939

As the Italians were spread throughout the South, they had became part of their local community. Naturally, they wanted to keep their Italian identity, and towns such as Pontypridd held an Italian school twice a week in order to keep the Italian language alive among the immigrants. However, the Italians faced problems during the Second World War. Wales was on the side of the Allies, while Italy was on the side of Hitler and Nazi Germany. Every Italian in Wales was a potential target as newspapers such as the *Daily Mirror* declared:

> **We are nicely honeycombed with little cells of potential betrayal.**

In some areas, there were attacks on Italian cafés and shops, but these were exceptions. Some tried to defend themselves, as the following advertisement shows:

MRS A VICCARI
of the Cosy Corner Café
86 DUNRAVEN STREET TONYPANDY
wishes to inform the public
that she is a
BRITISH SUBJECT
and has a brother now serving
in the British Army and also a
brother now serving in the British Navy.

Italian men were sent to camps under the direct orders of the government. On the other hand, the majority of people sympathised with their Italian neighbours. When Ernesto Melardi from Tonypandy was sent to a concentration camp, his wife was left in charge of their café. She could speak no Welsh and very little English, she had a five year old daughter and was expecting another child. She received a great deal of help from her neighbours, Mr and Mrs Rogers, and John Davies, who helped out in the shop. Eventually, the government gave in to the protests of other shopkeepers at Tonypandy, and Ernesto was released. When he returned to Tonypandy, as well as running the café, Ernesto also kept an eye out for fires. He was therefore helping the Allies' war effort!

One new group of Italians that arrived in Wales during the war were prisoners of war captured by the Allied armies and sent to camps in various parts of Wales. Such camps were to be found in many areas, including Ceredigion and Anglesey. After the war, many of the Italian men decided to remain in Wales.

Look at the extract from the *Daily Mirror* again. When reading about the experiences of Italians in Wales, would you agree that newspapers had a significant effect on people's attitudes?

The Docks

As you saw in the first chapter, there were many different nationalities living in the large ports of Wales. Some were well respected, such as Norwegian sailors, and they faced no difficulty in settling down locally. But things were not so easy for many other immigrants, despite their important contribution to the Welsh economy and society. Many of Cardiff's immigrants had seen little or no improvement in their lives since the riots of 1919. In 1929, a survey of businesses in Cardiff found that over 80% opposed employing black people. Many restaurants, hotels and dance halls also refused admission to black people. Butetown, however, was an area where people from many different nationalities lived side by side. It's estimated that there were as many as 50 different nationalities living there by the 1940s.

Roald Dahl, children's novelist from Cardiff and son of a Norwegian immigrant

Swansea Norwegian Church at its original site

Victor Parker, a popular jazz guitarist in Cardiff in the 30s and 40s, who continued playing until the 80s. He was of Afro-Caribbean descent.

Said Ismail Ali Shuqule. Originally from Somalia, he settled in Wales and fought with the Allies during the Second World War.

Riots

The Great Depression in 1930 hit Europe hard, and there were riots in Wales. White sailors believed that ship owners were favouring Arabs and Somalis when it came to choosing ship crews. And the Arabs and Somalis were angry because the Seamen's Union had reached an agreement with the ship owners to limit their use of Arab and Somali sailors. Towards the end of July, there was fighting in Swansea and, by August, in Cardiff. Weapons such as knives and clubs were used and the police had to be called to restore order.

The overall result of the riots of 1919 and 1930 was that ethnic minorities tended to stay together within their own community and didn't mix with the wider society. This provided them with some security. There were also advantages to settling down near friends and families.

The Yemeni

One community which prospered during this period was the Yemeni community. The port of Aden in North Africa was an important bunkering port for steam ships and it was Welsh coal that was used there. This is how the Yemeni turned to the sea for their livelihood and settled in ports such as Cardiff. Like many of the Welsh, the Yemeni were people from the countryside who went to sea in order to find work. The sailors from the Yemen usually worked as stokers in the engine room. This meant working long hours in hot, dirty and cramped conditions.

The first mosque in Britain – in Peel Street, Cardiff. The present mosque is on the same site but Peel Street no longer exists.

Many men from the Yemen came to Wales. After arriving in ports such as Cardiff, Swansea or Newport, they would stay in local lodging houses while waiting for their next ship. Some of the men met and married local women and stayed in Wales. Cardiff became a second home for many of them. As they settled in their new communities, they brought their own traditions with them. The first Arab mosque in Britain was opened in Cardiff in 1944. It was in Cardiff also that the first Arab newspaper in the British Isles was published, called *Al-Salam*.

Sport

As Butetown developed its own unique community, sport began to play an important part in people's lives, especially cricket and football. There is little evidence that they played against teams in the wider community at this time. By the 1930s, a local team, the Cardiff All Blacks, was playing charity football matches, and one member of the team was given a trial by Cardiff City F.C. In 1931, Eddie Paris, who was born in Chepstow and was black, played for Wales in an international football match against Ireland. On the other hand, many people believed that James Ernest, a black sailor from St. Lucia, was not allowed to play cricket for Glamorgan, nor Roy Francis rugby for Wales, because of racism.

 From the evidence on these two pages, list the difficulties faced by immigrants in Wales in their everyday lives.

James Ernest and his son Harry

Refugees

The Wall Street Crash in New York in 1929 led to the Great Depression. The depression had a world-wide effect and led to the growth of fascism in many European countries, and to war, including the Second World War.

The Basques

Between 1936 and 1939 there was a civil war in the Spanish state. On the one side were Franco and the Fascists, on the other the Republicans. Some of the Welshmen who fought on the Republican side were of Spanish descent. Others, such as Captain 'Potato' Jones, used his ship, the Marie Llewellyn, to help 800 people escape the fighting. J. Williams Hughes, who worked for the Red Cross in Madrid, gave weekly radio reports in Welsh on the war to people back home.

One of the worst events of the war was the attack on the town of Gernika in the Basque Country. Without any warning, German aircraft bombed the town, killing men, women and children. The Welsh were more than willing to help the Basques who, like the Welsh, were one of the oldest nations in Europe. Cambria House in Caerleon was opened to provide a home for the refugees, and other homes were opened in many parts of Wales, including Swansea, Old Colwyn and Brechfa. Lord Davies, Llandinam, the coal master, gave large sums of money to a fund set up to help the Basque children in Wales. The children also received help from the old Spanish communities at Aber-craf and Dowlais in Merthyr.

The Basque children contributed to Welsh life. They had their own magazine which they sold to the Welsh. They also had a very successful football team – the Basque Boys' Wonder Team. Local communities would take the Basque children on trips, and they were allowed to go to the cinema free. Although most of them returned to the Basque Country in 1941, some remained in Wales.

The Jews

The Jews were persecuted in Nazi Germany and some fled to Wales. British fascists also persecuted the Jews. Although there were a handful of fascists in Wales, there was very little support for them. Oswald Mosley, the leader of the British fascists, complained that Wales offered him very little support compared to parts of England. When one miner suggested that South Wales miners should attack Jewish shops, Arthur Horner, the miners' leader, made it clear he would resign if this happened.

Jewish immigration from Europe had a positive effect on the Welsh economy, with most businesses at Trefforest industrial estate being in Jewish hands by 1939.

The English

During the Second World War, many evacuees migrated from the large towns and cities of England to the Welsh countryside and the South Wales valleys. They received a warm welcome. In many of the Welsh speaking parts of Wales, some of the English immigrants learnt Welsh and settled down to spend the rest of their lives there. On the other hand, there were also cases of clashes between the local people and the evacuees.

In Carmarthenshire for example, there was tension between evacuees from the East End of London and the county's farmers. In some parts of North Wales, there was disagreement between Catholics from Liverpool and the chapelgoers of the Welsh countryside.

Evacuees arriving at Newtown Station in 1939

Freddie Grant, an evacuee from Liverpool, in Pen Llŷn during the Second World War

... and others

Of course, many other people fled from Europe during the war and settled in Wales. These included the Czecks in North Wales, the Poles in Pembrokeshire and the Wrexham area, and the Dutch in Holyhead. There were refugees from Germany, Austria and Czechoslovakia working in the North Wales forestries, and they were warmly received locally. Some of them organised international dances, and they had an international choir performing at Llangollen.

 Do the examples on these two pages show a change in attitude towards immigrants?

Compare and contrast

List the immigrants that moved to Wales during the period 1918-1945. List the ways in which their experiences were similar to each other and how they were different, for example:

- Why did the different groups move to Wales?
- Was each group welcomed in Wales?

Glossary

bunkering – *llwytho glo*, loading coal on board a ship for fuel

economic depression – *dirwasgiad economaidd*, a period of hardship and unemployment

identity – *hunaniaeth*, what makes someone the person he or she is and differentiates him or her from others

orthodox – *uniongred*, a word to describe someone or something which accepts or represents the official permitted and approved belief

pawnbroker shops – *siopau gwystlo*, shops which lend money, with added interest, in exchange for looking after items

rabbis – *rabïaid*, the Jewish religious leaders

violence – *trais*, hurting people physically

Chapter 3 1945-1990
Overview

The years immediately following the Second World War (1939–1945) were very difficult ones for the people of Wales because of economic hardship. During these years, many people remembered the poverty of the 1930s and there seemed no reason for people to move to Wales in large numbers.

By the 1960s, the standard of living of most people was improving. More people could afford motor cars and were able to go on holiday, and this meant that the population was much more mobile. This would certainly have an effect on Wales.

By the 1980s however, the closure of the coal mines, among other factors, meant that the old industries were in decline. On the other hand, there were now a number of new industries moving in to Wales. All these developments meant that many different types of immigrants were settling in Wales during the years 1945–90.

The English

Tourism was not something new in 20th century Wales. For example, many people from the industrial north-west of England had been spending their summer holidays on the coast of North Wales since the middle of the nineteenth century. Following the Second World War, there were new developments in tourism, such as the opening of Butlins holiday camp in Pwllheli in 1947. These developments attracted more tourists to Wales. As a result, many people began to move from the English cities to Wales permanently. By 1951, 20% of the population of Meirionethshire was born in England. Yet this county was one of the most rural in Wales, and the Welsh language was the first language of most of its people. Those who had moved to the towns and cities of Wales from England during the early years of the century had become part of the community, but those who moved to rural Wales after the Second World War tended to be much more isolated from the rest of the community.

Rural and coastal Wales saw a huge increase in immigration from England during the 1960s and 1970s. For example, Anglesey was transformed in the 1960s when industrial works were established at Holyhead, Wylfa Nuclear Power Station was built near Cemaes, and many coastal villages became holiday destinations. The population of the island increased substantially, with most of the immigrants coming from England in search of work, to retire or to buy a holiday home.

By the 1970s, the scale of immigration to rural Wales was raising controversial issues. One reason for this was the effect on the Welsh language. Before the war, the few who had settled in rural Wales had learnt the Welsh language and lived their lives through the medium of Welsh. But the mass immigration of the 1970s meant that the language of the communities was changing. Another problem was that those who retired from England could buy houses for prices that were beyond the reach of local people. In addition, certain areas of work led to substantial migration – for example, the majority of the academic staff at universities such as Bangor and Aberystwyth came from England. Also, the increase in the number of holiday homes was causing huge problems in several areas in Wales and threatening the Welsh language. One sign of the people's frustration was the campaign to burn holiday homes by Meibion Glyndŵr.

All these factors meant that relations between locals and immigrants were not always friendly.

'The history of Wales in the twentieth century is one of immigration from England on a very high scale, on a level far higher than that experienced by Scotland.' (R. Merfyn Jones in *Cymru 2000: Hanes Cymru yn yr Ugeinfed Ganrif*).

Why was there so much immigration from England to Wales? Was this an advantage for Wales?

A mixture of the old and the new

The Irish

The Irish were a long established immigrant group in Wales. But even during the 1950s, some still thought of themselves as Irish rather than Welsh. However, by this time, those of Irish descent had become more and more a part of the wider Welsh society. One possible reason for this is that there was far less Irish immigration during this period.

Dennis O'Neill, the world famous opera singer, is from Irish descent and fluent in Welsh

The Italians

The 1950s was a boom time for the Italian cafés. The coal industry flourished until the mid 1950s and the steel industry until the 1960s, so people had plenty of money to spend in the cafés!

However, during the 1960s there was a decline in the number of people visiting the cafés. There were many reasons for this. The economy of South Wales was declining and there were many social changes. More people could afford cars and more homes had a television. There was also a variety of entertainment available at drinking clubs and bingo halls. But the cafés did not disappear entirely, and improved transport made it easier for the Italian Welsh people to go to Italy on holiday. For example, since 1982 an annual 'Festival of the Emigrants' is held in Bardi in Italy to welcome the Italian Welsh who go 'home' to Italy for their holidays.

A new wave of Italians ... and others

Following the Second World War, there was a shortage of workers in many industries. Workers were recruited to Wales from Poland, the Ukraine, Ireland and Italy. The Poles and the Irish did not stay long in the tinplate industry and so, in the 1950s, 2,250 Italians were recruited from Napoli (Naples), Milano (Milan) and Genoa. They did not always receive a warm welcome. In Llanelli, for example, they stayed in hostels with other workers and this sometimes led to clashes over race or language. As the tinplate industry was in decline by the mid 1950s, many returned to Italy. Others stayed to work in the cafés or in other employment.

Stefan Terlezki (1927-2006), Conservative MP and Chairman of Cardiff City F.C, originally from the Ukraine

Toni Schiavone, campaigner for the Welsh language, of Italian descent

Gypsies and Travellers

The Gypsies had been an important part of Welsh life over many centuries, but there was still a lot of prejudice against them. This was despite some Gypsy families being famous in Wales, such as the Wood family.

By the 1970s and 1980s, new types of travellers could be seen in Wales which increased prejudice against Gypsies and all travellers. Many tinkers and 'new age travellers' faced problems when they tried to set up camp in different parts of Wales. Local people usually opposed their presence and this could sometimes lead to angry clashes. This happened when local councils tried to set up official sites for them in Swansea and Wrexham.

A Gypsy family near Bala, 1948

A new type of immigrant to Wales during this period was the hippy. Hippies came in search of remote rural areas where they could lead an alternative lifestyle. One of the most famous sites was Tepee Valley in West Wales. However, there were occasional clashes here too.

A Gypsy camp in the 1970s. The camp was created on the site of 'Little Ireland', where some of the poor Irish lived at one time.

Hippies near the village of Pont-rhyd-y-groes, Ceredigion, 1976

The Jews

Despite being a settled part of many Welsh communities, by the 1950s and 1960s many young Jews had left to look for work elsewhere. In contrast to the past, there were no Jewish immigrants to take their place. In 1951, the first issue of the magazine *CAJEX* was published, which aimed to link the Jewish community throughout South Wales.

On the whole, Jews in Wales had avoided the confrontation and racist attacks which had taken place in other parts of Europe. This was because they had been a part of the wider community in Wales. In 1987, for example, Cardiff appointed its first Jewish mayor. Although there were some racist incidents during this period, such as an attack on Jewish graves in a cemetery at Bryn-mawr in the early 1970s, these were exceptions.

Leo Abse, Labour MP of Jewish descent, 1970s

A painting by Josef Herman entitled Miner Bathing. *He had escaped from the Nazis in Poland, but lost his whole family to the concentration camps. He came to live in Ystradgynlais and spent his life painting the miners in the area.*

Dannie Abse, doctor and poet of Jewish descent, and brother to Leo Abse

How had the experiences of the Italians, the Gypsies, the Jews and the Irish changed between 1900 and 1990? How had their experiences remained the same during this period?

To Tiger Bay and beyond

The multicultural docklands

These photographs show the multicultural dockland area of Cardiff in the 70s. Many of these buildings would be demolished at a later date, destroying whole communities.

Prejudice against black people, Somalis and Arabs continued in ports such as Cardiff, Swansea and Newport after 1945. Discussions were held in the South Wales Coalfield in 1948 on the employment of black men underground, and there were arguments for and against.

In Tiger Bay, there lived a variety of communities consisting of, among others, Norwegians, the Japanese, the Chinese, Somalis, Bengalis, Afro-Caribbeans, Yemenis and, of course, the Welsh. Children in Tiger Bay would see other cultures around them every day. They would see different religious festivals celebrated on the streets. Tiger Bay was very different to the rest of Cardiff, and it was also much more multicultural than the rest of Wales. When the inhabitants of Tiger Bay moved outside their community, they expected racist attitudes towards them. One small sign of a change in attitude occurred in 1955 when students at Cardiff University protested against landlords who discriminated against black people.

Due to the Welsh economy facing so many problems after the Second World War, few people moved to Tiger Bay. Those who did were not always welcomed because the local community was now very stable and had gained a place in the city's life. They feared that new immigrants would harm the balance in the local community. Life for the inhabitants of Tiger Bay was difficult. Poor housing and poor job prospects were still a serious problem.

Multicultural Wales?

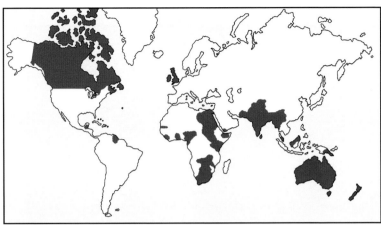

The British Empire

In the years following the Second World War, as the British Empire began to break up, the government tried to recruit people from the countries of the empire due to a shortage of workers in many industries and professions. So, many people from different parts of the world arrived in Wales looking for work. They were mostly Afro-Caribbeans, Indians, Pakistanis and Bangladeshis. By the 1960s, many people from the Commonwealth (the countries which once belonged to the British Empire) had come to live in Wales.

By the 1980s, more than 11,000 people who had been born in the Commonwealth were living in Wales. They did not settle solely in Tiger Bay but also in other parts of Cardiff and the rest of Wales. As a result, Cardiff now had a number of small communities of different nationalities. These communities had their own places of religious worship where they could speak their own language and

follow their own traditional way of life, side by side with the modern city life. One example of such immigrants were the Bhuttra Sikhs. There were only 300 Bhuttra Sikhs in Cardiff but they formed a small close-knit community, speaking their own language.

This new wave of immigrants did not just settle in Cardiff. They could be found in all parts of Wales. Some, for example, ran their own businesses, such as shops and restaurants. Others worked in the health service as doctors and nurses. Many others worked very long hours for very low pay in an attempt to ensure a new life for their families in their new homeland.

Prejudice and racism were major problems for these immigrants. Another problem was a lack of understanding of their needs. There were complaints, for example, that schools did not offer multicultural education. Wales also lacked social workers who could speak Asian languages. This was vital for anyone working with Asian communities.

Betty Campbell MBE. Her father was an immigrant from Jamaica in 1921 and was killed at sea during the Second World War. She was the first black person to be appointed head of a school in Wales. She is now a councillor in Butetown.

The Chinese

Although the Chinese usually ran laundries and restaurants, they also worked in other fields such as the health service. The main advantage of restaurants and laundries was that the family could work together. This was also a good way of ensuring that the language and traditions were passed on to the children. In contrast to other immigrants, the Chinese were spread out across Wales. They placed great emphasis on education in order to improve their lives and to move into vocations such as law and medicine.

Do history books such as the one that you are now reading help people from different ethnic groups to understand more about each other's history?

Refugees and asylum seekers

Poles after the war ...

One group of immigrants which was very prominent in Wales during the years following the Second World War were the Poles. Many had fled from Hitler during the war. Others had joined them after the war when Poland became communist and faced economic problems. The Welsh coal industry required more workers and 1,700 Poles arrived in the county of Flint. The same number arrived in Glamorgan. There were strong feelings against them for a while as it was felt that local workers should have been given the priority. But they slowly became accepted by the community. Many of the Poles who worked on farms soon learnt Welsh. In 1950, there was a march of 800 Poles and their families through the streets of Cardiff to express their identity within Wales.

... and others in the modern world

By the 1980s, one of the greatest problems facing the world was refugees. Due to wars, famine and extreme poverty in many different parts of the world, there were now many more refugees. Between 1980 and 1983 the number of refugees in the world increased from 5.7 million to 10.9 million.

The governments of the rich countries of the west thought that they had found an answer to the problem by the quota system. This meant that they would accept a certain number of refugees from various parts of the world at times of crisis. This allowed the government in London, for example, to control the number of refugees and to appear 'humanitarian.' As a result, the United Kingdom accepted 5,000 refugees from Chile in 1975 and 12,000 from Viet Nam between 1979 and 1984.

The government in London was also keen to disperse the refugees throughout the United Kingdom. So, for example, 602 Vietnamese lived in Wales in 1981. However, because people prefer to live near others of a similar background, the number had fallen to 282 by 1991 as many had moved to cities in England.

The Somalis

Refugees could also strengthen communities already established in Wales. Many men from Somalia had been a part of Cardiff life since the nineteenth century, when they came originally as sailors. Their aim was to earn a wage in order to provide for their families back home in Somalia. More Somali men moved to Wales in the 1950s in search of work, and by the 1960s they had been joined by their wives and children, who then settled in Cardiff. By the end of the 1960s, Cardiff had a Somali community. By the 1980s, the political situation in Somalia was threatening the lives of many people there. As there were already Somali communities in Cardiff and Newport, many moved there in order to get the support and security of members of the same community. One of the signs that the Somali community was developing was the establishing of the Somali Progressive Association in 1988 in response to the needs of the Somali community.

A Somali saying:

CARDIFF, MY HOME

But what about those refugees who came to Wales without a similar community waiting for them?

Dr Vaughan Robinson, Professor in Human Geography at Swansea University, has interviewed many of these people. Here is the story of one – Juan from Chile.

Juan was one of 5,000 people who came to Britain to escape from General Pinochet, the dictator of Chile. Juan had been in prison in Chile, but because Pinochet wanted good relations with the rest of the world, he had agreed to release prisoners. Juan believed that he would only be in Britain for a short time.

He had heard of Wales because, while he was a political prisoner in Chile, he had received letters from trade union members in Pontypridd. He thought that the Welsh names were very odd and believed that they were a secret code. Many of the prison guards thought the same! Having arrived in the United Kingdom, he was sent to Wales, to a town where others from Chile had also been sent. They spoke Spanish together and produced leaflets about Chile. As changes began to take place in Chile, many went home, including Juan. However, he realised that he had enjoyed living in Wales and so returned here.

Were refugees and asylum seekers during the period 1945-1990 different or similar to the following?:

1. Belgians arriving in Wales during the Great War (1914-1918)
2. Seamen from Somalia settling in Cardiff 1900-1945
3. Italians setting up businesses in Wales 1900-1945
4. Basques fleeing from Franco's forces 1936-1939
5. Evacuees from English towns and cities during the Second World War (1939-1945)
6. Hippies searching for a different way of life from the 1960s onwards

Culture and Sport

There were many developments in sport and culture in the decades following the Second World War. Many individuals from immigrant ethnic communities came to national attention in Wales. But this happened slowly and there was still a lot of prejudice.

In 1946, the Cardiff International Athletics Club was established by second generation immigrants from Butetown, many of whom had returned from the war and from the armed forces. They concentrated on rugby, and their style of play was exciting. They soon played across the whole of South Wales and abroad. But racism was not far from the surface.

Billy Boston was born in Tiger Bay to parents from Ireland and the West Indies, and he was a superb rugby and cricket player. But he soon realized that he would never play for Glamorgan or Wales and so turned to Rugby League to play for Wigan in the north of England. He became a hero there, scoring a total of 571 tries in 564 games! And he would not be the last to travel to the north of England to play Rugby League ...

Billy Boston, Great Britain winger, gets away with the ball during the Rugby League World Cup game between Australia and Great Britain, October 1960

The famous boxer Joe Erskine came from Butetown. His father came from the West Indies and his mother from a white Cardiff family that kept a lodging house for sailors. He became Champion of the British Empire in 1956.

However, Butetown was not the only place to produce leading sportsmen. Clive Sullivan, the first black rugby captain, came from Splott in Cardiff, and Hubert Best (Welsh mother and Jamaican father), from Milford Haven, played soccer for Cardiff. Clive Charles, born in Bow, London, was the first black player to captain Cardiff City F.C. He captained during 1973-74.

By the 1970s and 1980s, opportunities for ethnic minorities in the field of sports had improved, but they were still far from perfect. This was most obvious in rugby. The Welsh Rugby Union was willing to allow Wales to play against South Africa despite the fact that the government of South Africa followed a policy of apartheid. However, even though the South African tour in 1969-70 went ahead, including a game against Wales, several demonstrations and protests were held throughout the tour by people from every background, with the strongest protests happening at Swansea.

A major breakthrough happened in 1983 when Mark Brown became the first black man to play rugby for Wales. Born in Newport, he played for Pontypool, and he played six times for Wales between 1983 and 1986. This paved the way for other black players to represent Wales. However, there were still problems. In 1987, there was an incident at a game between Cardiff and Aberafan Quinns when Gerald Cordle, a Cardiff player, and a supporter started fighting because the supporter had been shouting racist abuse at Cordle.

Slowly, people from different backgrounds also came to be accepted in the field of popular entertainment in Wales. The most famous singer was probably Shirley Bassey, who became world renowned. Her success won admiration throughout Wales because of her Welsh background in Tiger Bay. Ethnic music, such as reggae, also influenced Wales from the 1970s onwards.

Shirley Bassey

One of the most progressive groups in Wales was the Welsh language band Geraint Jarman a'r Cynganeddwyr, which played rock and reggae. The group consisted of a Welsh-speaking Welshman, non Welsh-speaking Welshmen, an Englishman, a Welsh Italian and a Welsh Chinese-Caribbean.

However, these examples still did not mean that Wales had created a multicultural society which offered equality to all members of Wales' immigrant communities.

Aaron Ahmun, the Welsh Chinese-Caribbean drummer, who was a member of Geraint Jarman a'r Cynganeddwyr

Did the success of individuals from among the immigrants in sport and culture help immigrants to be accepted by the rest of society?

Continuity and Change
1. List the ethnic groups which moved to Wales during the twentieth century.
2. How did the experiences of these groups change as the century progressed?
3. How had the experiences of these groups not changed during the century?

Glossary
apartheid – *apartheid*, a policy of separating people because of their race
disperse – *gwasgaru*, to scatter
humane – *dyngarol*, to love fellow humans and to show it by doing something to help them

Chapter 4 The 1990s

Overview

The opening of the National Assembly for Wales in 1999 was a clear sign of Welsh identity to the world. It was an important turning point in Welsh history. But, not one member of an ethnic minority group was elected to the first ever National Assembly. However, the Assembly made it clear that it was to pay attention to the needs of all the people of Wales and that there was room for all to contribute to the new Wales. The success of people from different ethnic backgrounds in different fields in Wales was a sign that Wales was a multicultural country. But this did not mean that people from all ethnic backgrounds were given equal respect or equal social rights. There was still some way to go.

Ethnic immigrants have influenced eating habits in Wales

'Yesterday's immigrants have become today's Welsh'

As the people of Wales have become more aware that people from all ethnic backgrounds are a part of Welsh life, it has made them think about what makes a person Welsh. Wales is a country of people from different cultures, races, religions and languages, and society is changing and developing quickly. For example, one generation which has moved to Wales may feel that their first loyalty is to their mother country – England, Bangladesh, Italy or Somalia. Their children, who have been born and/or have grown up in Wales, may feel themselves to be part of two nations – Wales and the homeland of their parents.

The history of the South Wales valleys shows this change. At the beginning of the twentieth century there was a huge influx into the valleys because the industries there attracted people from many parts of the world. By the end of the century, these areas had the highest percentage of people born in Wales living there. As the historian Merfyn Jones points out:

'Yesterday's immigrants have become today's Welsh.'

People from various ethnic backgrounds socialising and enjoying themselves at the Cardiff MAS Carnival, 1999. The carnival is an annual event.

1. What does Merfyn Jones mean?
2. Do you agree with him?
3. If this is the case, was Wales truly multicultural at the end of the twentieth century?
4. Had attitudes changed by the end of the century?

The English

The most significant ethnic group in terms of numbers and influence to move to Wales are the English. This continued in the final decade of the century due to immigration to rural Wales and to the coast. For many people, the coast of North Wales was the 'Costa Geriatrica' because so many people, most of them retiring from the north-west of England, had moved to live there. They were attracted by the beautiful views and the fact that they were not far from their families in the north-west of England. The fact that many people from a similar background to them were living locally also appealed to them. On average, house prices in England were higher than those in Wales, which meant that they could buy a similar property in Wales cheaper.

Janet Ryder, AM for Plaid Cymru/The Party of Wales. An Englishwoman, she moved to Wales from Sunderland in 1990.

However, not everyone moved to Wales to retire. For example, many people moved to live in north-east Wales and then travelled to England every day to their work. Others had moved to Wales to begin a new life with their families in order to escape from city life in England.

Were the reasons why the English moved to Wales in the 1990s similar or different to the reasons why other ethnic groups moved to Wales during the century?

The old economy and the new economy – old immigrants and new immigrants

The Welsh economy changed during the final years of the twentieth century. Traditional Welsh industries such as coal and steel all but disappeared. New industries were attracted to Wales, especially new technological industries.

Many new factories opened in Wales, in the South and north-east for example. Many of them were established by companies from Japan, South Korea, the USA and Europe. These companies usually sent their own management teams to run the factories, with local people working in them. Certain key work areas also continued to attract workers from outside Wales. For example, the staff of many hospitals in Wales came from all parts of the globe, and universities also attracted staff and students from several continents.

A hospital health worker. People from different ethnic backgrounds are important to the Welsh health services.

The Japanese

Although small in number, one significant new ethnic group came to Wales at the end of the century. By the 1990s, there were more Japanese people living in Wales than in any other country in Europe. This was because Japanese managers of factories tended to bring their families with them. This is why the Emperor of Japan visited Cardiff in 1998 – the only other city in Britain that he visited outside London.

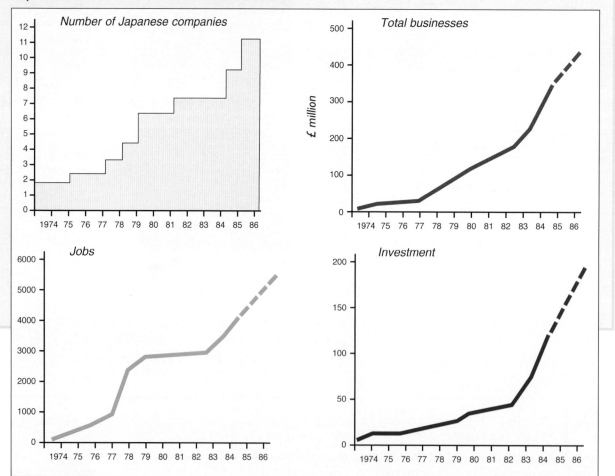

Japanese companies in Wales 1974-1986

The Italians

By the 1990s there were fewer and fewer Italian cafés in Wales. This did not mean that Wales had lost her Italian population. Many stayed in Wales and had summer homes in Italy. But they did face one problem. Sometimes the Welsh referred to them as Italians while, when they were in Italy, they were called Welsh or English. On the other hand, they felt very privileged to be part of two cultures and had strong feelings for both. This is what a lady called Iolanda Rossi, who lives at Ebbw Vale, said:

"When I leave Bardi I cry; when I leave Ebbw Vale I cry".

The historian Colin Hughes has studied the history of the Italians in South Wales. He believes that they were accepted by the communities there. The main reason for this was that they set up businesses which did not threaten the livelihood of the local people. The nature of cafés also meant that local people spent a lot of time in them and so came to know the owners well. For many people, the Italians were good, kind and honest people. They were also spread across South Wales, living among the Welsh. Establishing the cafés coincided too with a period of prosperity in the South.

This photograph is very simple but it's also a significant source. It shows an advertisement on the window of Massari's Café in Cross Keys in 1986 (the Massaris were an Italian family).

Robert Sidoli, Cardiff Blues. An international rugby player of Italian descent.

Carlo Rizzi, an Italian who has learnt Welsh. He was the Musical Director of the Welsh National Opera between 1992 and 2001.

1. Do you agree with Colin Hughes's interpretation of the experiences of Italians in twentieth century Wales?
2. Were the experiences of Italians in Wales similar or different to the experiences of other groups which moved to Wales?

Multicultural Wales?

According to the 1991 Census, the number of people from ethnic minority groups in Wales were as follows:

Black (British):	7,660
Indians	6,384
Pakistanis	5,717
Chinese	4,801
Bangladeshis	3,820
Asian – Other	3,677
Black – Other	3,473
Black – Caribbean	3,348

The statistics show that Wales was a multicultural country even if the numbers from minority ethnic groups were small. If we add the above numbers together, the minority ethnic groups were only 1.5% of the total poplulation of Wales. The statistics do not tell us if their standard of living compared favourably with the rest of the population of Wales. The statistics also tell us nothing about the attitudes towards them.

Research has showed that much more needs to be done to ensure equality for ethnic minority groups in Wales. They usually live in poorer housing and are less likely to get good jobs. One result of establishing the National Assembly for Wales is that the Assembly has a duty to respect the needs of all people in Wales and to respond to their needs. But this would not happen overnight. Ethnic minority communities would have to rely mainly on their own communities' support in the meantime.

The Somalis

As we have already seen, the Somali population in Wales was an old established community, and it was still growing. By 1994 there were around 4,000 Somalis living in Cardiff, with over half of them having just arrived as refugees. They were a strong community because they came from the same part of Somalia. In our modern technological age, it's much easier for communities like the Somalis to keep in contact with their home communities. In the same way, Welsh speakers all over the world are able to listen to Radio Cymru and to read the news in Welsh through the BBC website, *Cymru'r Byd*.

The Somalis who had just arrived in Wales faced serious problems. They had escaped from civil war and were therefore refugees. But the government in London wanted to limit the number of asylum seekers. This meant that the Somalis found it difficult to gain entry for their wives and children. They wanted to help themselves but found it difficult due to the language problem which prevented them from getting assistance and from setting up their own businesses.

The Chinese

The case of the Chinese in Wales was different as they were distributed across the country. Many Chinese left Hong Kong in 1996 because they were afraid of Communist China. They went to many different countries across the world. In Wales, they wished to protect their identity within the wider community. For example, the Chinese of North Wales celebrated the Chinese New Year with a dinner. This included traditional singing, the Dragon Dance and the Lion Dance. Local dignitaries who were not Chinese were also invited. In many communities in Wales, the Chinese made sure that their children grew up trilingual – speaking their mother tongue, English and Welsh.

Religions

By the end of the twentieth century there had been a serious decline in the number of people who went to Protestant (church and chapel), Catholic and Jewish religious services. But there was a greater variety within the Christian faith. There was also a great variety outside the Christian faith – Bahaism, Buddhism, Hare Krishna, Hinduism, Sikhism and, especially, Islam (Muslim). These groups were to be found in all parts of Wales to a greater or lesser degree.

By the end of the twentieth century, the Muslim faith in particular was growing in Wales. Muslim communities could be found in Cardiff, Swansea, Newport, Bridgend and Rhondda Cynon Taf. By 1997, the Association of Muslim Professionals had been established in Wales. In urban districts, the tendency was for Muslims to live in one area where they could work, trade and worship. One advantage to this was that they could avoid racial or religious confrontations with other groups. But this did not mean that they always succeeded in avoiding such conflicts.

 A multicultural country has people of different races, languages, religions and cultures living side by side. From the evidence on these two pages and in the rest of this chapter, do you think that Wales was a multicultural country by the end of the twentieth century?

Refugees and asylum seekers

 Study the following map carefully. What does the map reveal about asylum seekers in Wales in 2004?

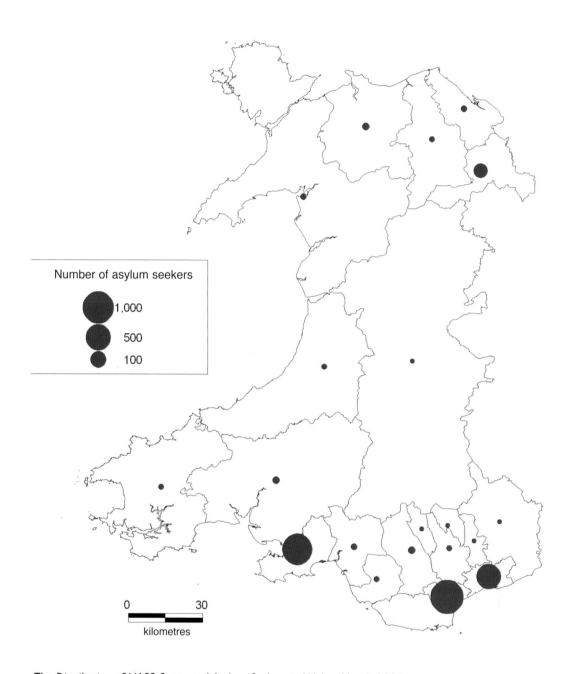

Number of asylum seekers

1,000

500

100

0   30
kilometres

The Distribution of NASS Supported Asylum Seekers in Wales, March 2004

As we saw in Chapter 3, there were many more refugees and asylum seekers in Wales from the 1970s onwards. Although Britain had agreed to accept a number of refugees during the period 1954-1991, the quota system meant that the numbers which arrived in the UK were limited. By the 1990s, the quota system was not working. Refugees were not waiting for the system to work. They were fleeing to another country and then claiming asylum when they arrived there. The result was an increase in those seeking asylum. More than 80,000 asylum seekers arrived in Britain in the year 2000 (but this was nothing compared to the 1.9 million refugees who arrived in Iran in 1999).

What were people's attitudes towards asylum seekers? On a British level, many newspapers claimed that there were too many of them. They claimed that they came here in order to take advantage of the services available, such as the health service. Opinion polls showed that most British citizens agreed with this. Newspapers in Wales were not so negative in their views. Welsh politicians also showed a more positive attitude. On the other hand, newspapers and politicians were slow to educate the public. They failed to explain why people had been forced to flee their country. Also, the newspapers did not always show asylum seekers as individuals.

Here is the story of Maria, a Kurd from Iran:

Maria's father was a member of the Kurdish Democratic Party. He received a tip-off that the government of Iran was going to arrest him. Maria and her family succeeded in escaping to Turkey. They were afraid to ask for official help to come to Britain, where they had family living already. They feared that the government of Iran would know where they were and would prevent them leaving or even kill them. Eventually, an agent got them to Britain illegally at a cost of £5,000 each. When they reached Britain, the agent escaped with their papers.

The family applied for asylum and moved to Wales, where Maria's brother lived. They had not realised that Wales was a different country, with its own language and culture. They felt that Wales was much more welcoming than London. Maria was angry with the immigration system which wanted proof that they were being persecuted.

Maria came from a wealthy Iranian family. She had a university degree. In Wales, she worked in a pizza shop until she got a job in the health service. She is pleased to be in Wales and enjoys the right to freedom of speech here. However, she points out:

'We are here because we just want to save our lives, you know. Nothing else. Not because we are interested to be in another country. We love our country … We love Kurdistan.'

List the countries from which the refugees/asylum seekers came. Use the internet and/or history books to find out what was happening in these countries in the 1980s and 1990s. Why do you think that these people left their homeland?

Racist Wales?

The 1991 census showed that 1.5% of the population of Wales belonged to ethnic minorities.

> In 1994 28% of black men of Caribbean origin were unemployed.
> In 1994 35% of other black men were unemployed.
> In 1994 11% of white men were unemployed.
> In 1994 up to 500 racist attacks took place in South Wales.

 What do these statistics tell us about multicultural Wales?

By the 1990s, people in Wales were more willing to discuss racist attitudes. It was obvious that Wales was multicultural, but there was still an element of racism present.

Following an argument over the sale of bread, an Asian shop was attacked in Ely, Cardiff in 1991. This led to riots, but it appears that the riots were mainly anti-police and that the cause was poverty. These riots were not like the riots of 1911 or 1919.

In 1994 Mohan Singh Kullar was killed in Cadoxton near Neath. He kept a shop and had gone outside to investigate a group of young men who were drunk and causing trouble. A brick was thrown at him and he died. One of the young men was sentenced to life imprisonment.

Such incidents did raise questions regarding the nature of Welsh racism and the extent to which Wales was racist.

Various right wing groups did exist in Wales, such as the BNP and Combat 18. Some of these groups were responsible for the racist violence in Wales. Nick Griffin, leader of the BNP, came to live in Wales in 1990. Alan Belshella, an American who was a member of the Ku Klux Klan, moved to live near Maesteg in the 1980s.

But these were only extreme examples. There was little support for extremist parties in elections. In the General Election of 1979, for example, the extremist parties only received 2,465 votes out of a total of 1,636,788 votes. The situation had not changed by the 1990 – in an election in Cardiff North in 1992, the BNP candidate received 121 votes, only 0.3% of the total votes cast.

Racial incidents reported to the police

Police Area	1988	1994-95	1995-96	1996-97	1997-98
Dyfed/Powys	0	3	23	18	17
Gwent	1	22	32	60	45
North Wales	2	3	5	4	12
South Wales	86	512	443	357	367

It is difficult to draw conclusions from such tables. For example, far more people lived in South Wales than in Dyfed/Powys. Also, it's more than likely that people who faced racism on a day by day basis did not report such incidents to the police. But the fact that people were at last willing to report racial incidents showed a change in attitude. No such figures exist for the beginning of the twentieth century because the authorities did not see the problem at the time.

A journalist called Steve Evans summed up racism in the South Wales valleys by saying that it came from areas where there was a lot of unemployment and where some Asian British or Black British immigrants lived, who were quite well off. They had jobs as doctors or shopkeepers and so appeared very wealthy compared to unemployed locals.

This is what some people who claimed to be racist said:

> 'There's white people on the dole, when there's black people … owning restaurants and working as doctors and taking all the money when white people should be.'

On the other hand, the historian Neil Evans states that most people in the valleys were not racist. They were disgusted by the racism of the few. Some of those who suffered racial abuse argued that they received a lot of local support. Some local people were willing to stand up to racists. In Porth, the Rhondda, one white youth was willing to defend an Asian restaurant owner who was being abused. The youth was stabbed and subsequently died.

 Is poverty the main cause of racism?

The Welsh of today

By the 1990s, many more people from ethnic communities could be seen on Welsh sports fields, and several represented Wales in various sports. Many could also be seen in other cultural spheres.

Ali Yassine, an actor and presenter who works through the medium of Welsh and English

Jason Mohammad, a correspondent and presenter for BBC Cymru Wales who works through the medium of Welsh and English

Bernice Reubens, a novelist of Jewish descent

Trezza Azzopardi, a novelist from Cardiff's Maltese community

Lembit Öpik, born in Ireland, of Estonian descent and MP for Montgomeryshire

There was a small but steady increase in the number of ethnic rugby players who represented Wales. These included Glenn Webbe, Colin Charvis and Nigel Walker. Walker was particularly interesting as he was an athlete who turned to rugby. He also represented a change in attitude towards people from diverse ethnic backgrounds as he later became head of sport at BBC Cymru Wales.

As rugby became professional and more international, players from different parts of the world came to play rugby in Wales. This did not mean that racism disappeared completely from the rugby pitch, but the contribution of players from many different ethnic backgrounds was now more obvious.

The same was true in the world of football. Ryan Giggs was the son of Rugby League player Danny Wilson and was very proud of his African roots. Robbie Earnshaw from Zambia and Nathan Blake played football for Cardiff and for Wales. Players from different ethnic backgrounds also played in the Welsh Premiership, for example Sammy Ayorinde played for Bangor City and Nigeria.

Nathan Blake

People's ethnic background became less of a problem in other sports too, as the successes of the boxer Steve Robinson and the athlete Colin Jackson show. Cricket also had players from several different backgrounds.

There were many reasons for the change in attitude. People from different ethnic backgrounds were becoming more accepted by society as a whole. Sport brought people from all parts of the world to play in Wales and so people now looked out to the world more than in the past. By the 1990s, people from different ethnic backgrounds could be found in all parts of Wales. Not one of the sportsmen named on this page were originally from Butetown. Times had changed.

Joe Calzhage, boxing champion. Born in England, his mother came from Wales and his father from Sardinia.

The contribution of people from different backgrounds was not confined to sport. For example, in the field of pop music, one sign of the cross-over between different cultures could be seen on the album *Stwff* by Llwybr Llaethog, which includes songs in Welsh, English, Scots Gaelic and Punjabi. One of the most popular groups to sing in English on Sain's Welsh record label was One Style, a reggae band from England. In the arts, India Dance Wales was established in 1993 by Kiran Ratna, a professional dancer specializing in Bharata Natyam. And the film *Solomon & Gaenor* was nominated for an Oscar. This film was in three languages (Welsh, English and Yiddish) and it had the 1911 riots as its background.

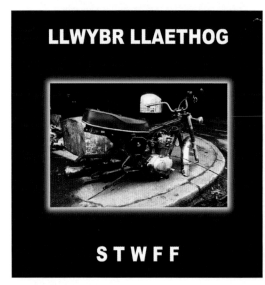

Stwff by Llwybr Llaethog

Sirajul Islam with the presenter Nia Parry on the Welsh medium programme Nôl i Fangladesh (Back to Bangladesh). Originally from Bangladesh, Sirajul Islam speaks Welsh and has established several restaurants in Swansea and Cardiff.

The group One Style

Charlotte Williams, author of Sugar and Slate, in which she shares her experiences of having a Welsh mother and a father from Guyana in the West Indies

India Dance Wales

A scene from Solomon & Gaenor

Dafydd Hughes, who works through the medium of Welsh with children with learning disabilities

Jerry Hunter, a scholar and author from the USA who works through the medium of Welsh and English

All this may show that Wales was facing its multicultural past in a world which was much more multicultural.

Apart from the individuals mentioned in this book, can you name other immigrants from different ethnic backgrounds who have enriched the life of Wales during the twentieth century?

Significance:

What do you consider to have been the significance of immigrants to the history of 20th century Wales?

Glossary

equality – *cydraddoldeb*, to be equal to everyone else
significance – *arwyddocâd*, importance
turning point – *trobwynt*, a time when an important change takes place

A CHANCE TO REFLECT

Now that you have read some of the history of immigrants to Wales during the twentieth century, the best way to conclude is by thinking about the following questions. By discussing these questions, we may be able to answer a very important question in the new century:

Has Wales become a country where all who live here feel that they belong and can contribute to the country's future?

1. Why did people move to Wales?

Here are some of the reasons why people move from one country to another. Are any of these true of the immigrants to Wales during the twentieth century?

- Looking for work
- Escaping from war
- Being persecuted in another country
- Searching for a better life
- Falling in love
- Following family or friends who have already migrated
- Migrating temporarily due to unemployment in their own country
- The nature of their work moving them from one part of the world to another
- Religious persecution

Can you think of other reasons?

Do any of these reasons also explain why some people moved from one part of Wales to another, and from Wales to other countries?

2. Arriving in Wales

- Did some regions in Wales attract immigrants more than other areas? Explain your answer.
- What problems faced those who had migrated to Wales?
- How did local people respond to immigrants?
- What did the immigrants think of Wales?
- Which groups of immigrants had a long history of immigration to Wales and which groups were new to Wales in the twentieth century?

3. The contribution of immigrants

- How did immigrants contribute to life in Wales during the twentieth century? Try to divide your answer under the following headings: political, social, economic and cultural.
- How did immigrants change life in Wales during the twentieth century? Try to divide your answer under the following headings: political, social, economic and cultural.
- Which immigrant would you choose as a Welsh Hero? Explain your choice.

4. Recording the history of all immigrant groups

- Why is the history of some immigrant groups during this period so rich, while there is very little information about other groups?
- Are there any immigrant groups which have not been included in this book? Suggest reasons for this.
- How can you find out more about the immigrant communities of Wales during the twentieth century?